Are You My Type?

Or Why Aren't You More Like Me?

Claudine G. Wirths
Mary Bowman-Kruhm

Illustrations by Ed Taber

CPP BOOKS
Palo Alto, California
A Division of Consulting Psychologists Press, Inc.

Myers-Briggs Type Indicator and MBTI are registered trademarks of Consulting Psychologists Press.

Library of Congress Cataloging-in-Publication Data
Wirths, Claudine G.
    Are you my type? : temperament typing for teens / Claudine G. Wirths,
Mary Bowman-Kruhm.
        p.   cm.
    Includes bibliographical references.
    Summary: An introduction to temperament and psychological type theory,
discussing its usefulness in understanding ourselves and others better.
    ISBN 0-89106-055-3
    1. Typology (Psychology)--Juvenile literature. 2. Myers-Briggs Type Indicator--
Juvenile literature. [1. Typology (Psychology) 2. Myers-Briggs Type Indicator.]
I. Bowman-Kruhm, Mary. II. Title.
BF698.3.W57 1992   92-20678
155.2'64--dc20   CIP
                                                                         AC

Printed in the United States of America

First edition
  First printing 1992

96 95 94 93   10 9 8 7 6 5 4 3 2

Dedicated to
Carl L. Kruhm, Jr.,
whose interest in type inspired us

Contents

Chapter Five
NT—Understanding and Knowing

Chapter Six
Making the Best of Yourself in School

Chapter Seven
Finding the Best in Others

Selected Resources

About the Authors

Preface

"Your assignment for tomorrow is to write a two-page paper on the future of teenagers in the twenty-first century!" announces your social studies teacher.

The minute class is over, would you most likely

- Start talking with friends about the neat things the future holds for kids?

- Drop the paper the assignment is written on in your hurry to get out of that boring class?

- Start adjusting your afternoon schedule to make room for a trip to the library?

- Tuck the assignment away to think about later since right now your mind is on your science project?

No matter which way you choose, you'll find this book has something to say that will help you understand not only why you made that choice but why you make the other choices you do in your life.

Traditionally, there have been two schools of thought on how to understand yourself and others. Some psychologists and scholars have promoted looking at the uniqueness of each of us. Others have focused on how much we are all alike.

In this book, we'll look at one approach to studying how people are alike—*temperament typing.* Temperament typing is a method many people find useful as a shorthand way to better understand themselves and others. We'll tell you about four common life patterns, or temperaments, and help you decide which one *you* are. You'll meet four very different teens, one of each of the four temperaments, and see how they get along with their parents, teachers, and friends. We'll talk about how kids of each temperament learn, how they play, and what things they value—plus much, much more!

If you're interested in finding out more about your own temperament and how temperament typing can help you every day, read on! We can tell you this—no one temperament is better than another. That's for sure.

Chapter One

Typecasting

This above all: to thine own self be true.
William Shakespeare, *Hamlet,* I, iii

Before talking about temperament types and how ideas about this theory can help you, let's clear up one possibly confusing term we'll be using—*temperament.* From the earliest times, typing people has been tied to the concept of temperament.

Does it have the same meaning as "temperamental"?

No. When we speak of someone as *temperamental,* we mean they are hard to get along with because they're very emotional and unpredictable and often moody. When we talk about *temperament,* we are talking about the unique behavior pattern that each human being seems to have from the time of birth.

If we're born with it, do we keep that temperament all through life?

Yes and no. Some psychologists believe that our temperament pattern is built-in and that we carry it within us throughout life.

1

Others are not so sure about the built-in nature…but whatever the case may be, our temperament characteristics help to make us act as we do unless we choose to act otherwise.

Are you saying we can't change our temperament?

Even though we can change some of the ways we express our tendencies, we don't seem able to really change our temperament. For example, children who are basically organized tend to remain organized throughout their lives. They seem to know where their socks and schoolwork and lunch money are without any effort at all. When they are grown, they keep a careful calendar and always hang their clothes in the proper place. Others who are not by temperament organized may have to work hard their entire lives to keep track of their belongings. Because they see that being organized is important, they make themselves behave in a way different from their basic temperament.

When you talk about how permanent temperament is, it reminds me of what my mom says: "Never date someone with the idea that you'll change them after you start going together."

Exactly. If a guy mistreats his girlfriend before they go steady, he will likely keep on doing that. If a girl pretends to like cars because she knows her boyfriend loves them, she will keep on pretending as long as she wants to be with him. But on the other hand, the person who comes on as strong and steady will probably stay strong and steady.

I have an aunt who seems to have changed. She talks about how she was a real teacher's pet when she was a kid. She says she squealed on all the other kids, never got punished for doing anything wrong, got straight A's, and was considered the perfect student. But when she was about forty, she suddenly left her husband and moved to Alaska. She got a job tending bar in a remote town, and she told us she was a new woman. That sounds as if she changed her temperament as well as the way she acts.

Your aunt probably had parents who were very forceful and strong.

How did you know? That's exactly right!

Sometimes parents can so dominate a child that it takes a lot of growing up on the part of the child before he or she listens to the feelings and urges inside them. Because of love for parents, fear of punishment, or desire to please, the child will repress his or her true feelings. We bet if you ask your aunt, she will tell you that as a child she had fantasies of being very different from the way she actually acted.

Are you saying that her temperament was there all the time?

Probably so. Your aunt would probably have been happier had she listened to her inner self earlier in life.

I'd sure hate to go halfway through life before I found out what I'd be happy doing!

To help you know better who you really are, school guidance counselors and teachers give career interest surveys and other questionnaires to help you analyze yourself and look at lots of options that are open to you. They believe one of the tasks of being a teenager is discovering what your temperament is and how best to act on it. If you don't live and work in a way that matches your temperament, you'll be stressed and unhappy a lot of the time.

So if I find out about my temperament, it can help me understand myself, why I act as I do, and how I can be more satisfied with life by listening to my inner self?

Yes. We hope to give you some basic information and ideas in this book. We also think this book will give you a different way of looking at other people in your life as well as yourself.

**You just said something that makes me curious....
I have a good friend who is so different from me that people ask us how we manage to get along. One of us is neat, the other is a slob; one of us is always on time, the other is always late; and so on. We like each other's company, but we bug each other sometimes. Are you saying that he's probably a different temperament from me and that it's just as natural for him to do things his way as it is for me to do things my way?**

You said it exactly. That is one of the most important things type can tell you. You learn not only that people are very different, but, by knowing the characteristics of their nature, you can learn how to get along with them a lot easier. (Or you'll learn how to *really* annoy them! Just kidding.)

If you know one or two major characteristics of a person's temperament, you can often make an assumption, or educated guess, about some of their other characteristics. For example, someone who has difficulty expressing close feelings may also tend to ignore birthdays and anniversaries.

This sounds like stereotyping to me. I really believe that stereotyping is bad because it leads to things that may not be true about other people. Those educated guesses you talked about can be totally wrong.

Good point. You have put your finger on one aspect of all this where you really have to be careful. Just because most people of a particular temperament show a certain pattern of characteristics, not everyone shows all the characteristics. In fact, although most of us are predominantly one type, we also show characteristics of one or more of the other types. Temperament typing offers us useful guidelines, not personality profiles cast in stone!

Then I'm not sure how typing people can be useful to me.

Here's an example of how you might use it. Suppose you want to concentrate on the lecture in your history class, but another student is driving you nuts by constantly talking to friends during class. If you know about temperament, you understand that the way the talker acts is as natural and ingrained to her as your way of settling down to listen is to you. Given that person's temperament, you realize you can't *make* that person stop just because you say, "Please stop talking." That student wouldn't pay attention even if the teacher told her to stop.

What you can do is negotiate with her to change her behavior. Tell her you want to stay friends, but that her constant chatter is driving you crazy. Because her type also values friendship, that person would probably be more willing to change, and it might work—at least for a while!

With all the different possibilities for human behavior, figuring out what temperament type someone is sounds like a pretty complicated job.

When characteristics are grouped, scholars of temperament typing, beginning with Hippocrates way back in 450 B.C., have discovered that they tend to cluster into four main groups.

There are millions of people in the world and I can't believe that every single person can fit into one of four groups.

If the idea of everyone's being crammed into only four groups bothers you, you may be interested to know that some typologists break each of those four into four more groups and end up with sixteen types. The *Myers-Briggs Type Indicator*®, for example, can tell you which of the sixteen types you are. That's a bit much, however, for us to cover here.

In this book we will use the four groups in the same way they are used by a psychologist named David Keirsey. He referred to the groups by letters: SP, SJ, NF, and NT. (We'll explain what the letters mean later.) The SP likes action, makes decisions quickly, and needs freedom. The SJ believes rules were meant to be followed, is dependable, and needs to belong. The NF likes people, is generally upbeat, sees good in almost every human, and needs to feel honest. The NT, who thinks and wonders and considers in order to understand ideas, needs to be competent.

We'll explain each of these temperaments in more detail in the chapters that describe them. For even more information, you may want to read other books of people who have studied in this field. We've listed some of them in the back of this book.

Even so, grouping into a few types doesn't seem possible. There are so many different *kinds* of people: crazy people and smart people, people who are unselfish and helpful and those who rip you off. You know what I mean?

Someone who is unselfish can be the same temperament type as someone who rips you off. Let's look at an example of the type we call SP. One of the characteristics of an SP is acting swiftly—making quick decisions and moving on them. A person with this nature can be a race driver, a firefighter, a mother who enjoys playing tag with her children as if she's a kid herself, a quarterback on the football team, President of the United States—or a tricky drug dealer!

Oh, I see. Two people can have the same drive, but they drive off in different directions!

Hey, that's pretty good! You're exactly right!

So can I figure out what my temperament is now?

Not yet. There's one other thing you need to know about why people of the same temperament can seem very different. No matter what your temperament, if you are the kind of person who tends to look outside yourself for what interests you—to other people and other things—you are called an *extravert*. If you are the kind who turns inward into your own world of ideas, you are called an *introvert*.

You can see how this could make two people who are the same temperament seem very different. In the SP examples we gave, the race driver could well be an introvert. When he races, he is happy to be all alone in that car, planning each exciting move in his head. However, the mother who likes to play tag with her children is probably an extravert. She wants to be racing around with other people even if they are much younger.

You mean like this friend of mine who goes out with us to parties now and then, but we've noticed he usually prefers to stay home?

Yes, by temperament he most likely enjoys being alone or with only one or two others. He may join in sometimes because he believes being friendly is important, but we bet he is one of the first to leave a party. It's unlikely that he will ever be a real party person because he is an introvert.

As with other sides of our temperament, we are not likely to change from being an introvert to an extravert or vice-versa. We can, however, change some of the ways we express ourselves. People who are shy by nature may always feel somewhat shy, but they can learn to behave in ways that hide their shyness. People who take the lead in meeting new people at a party can relax alone with a book—at least for a while.

Unless you have more questions, let's get going so you can figure out what temperament type you might be.

I'm ready!

Good. We've asked a person of each temperament to sit down and talk with us about how they feel. All you have to do is listen in on our conversations. When you get to the one where you keep saying, "Oh yeah. I know how that feels!" or, "Wow, that's me!" or, "That explains why I act that way," you'll pretty much know you have pinpointed your type.

Don't worry when you find that some parts of other descriptions fit you, too. Almost everyone has developed some abilities from the other temperaments as well.

Of course, listening in on all four conversations will help you identify the temperaments of other people in your life. When we finish talking about each of the four temperaments, we'll suggest some ways to use what you have learned about yourself and others. But now, listen while we talk to an SP.

Chapter Two

SP
Acting and Impacting

All the world's a stage.

William Shakespeare, *As You Like It,* II, vii

The **S** means that you use your **S**enses of seeing, hearing, feeling, tasting, and smelling to take in facts and information. The **P** means that you use **P**erception in dealing with your world; that is, you like to scan the world around you in an ongoing search for information to help you choose what to do in your present situation. You prefer keeping your options open rather than closing them off. The characteristics of this combination make you an **SP** who is action-oriented and focuses on what's happening *now.*

Sounds like me. Hey, I just thought of a way to remember the four temperaments. I can turn the letters SP, NT, NF, and SJ into a mnemonic: "Sarah's Pale 'cause Sam's in Jail and Nina's Flipped over Nick's Tricks." Now that I've got that much mastered, let's move on to something else.

That takes care of what type you are! You are most likely an SP. Life for you is wrapped up in the here and now. You tend to be easily bored, you are quick to change the subject if you aren't interested, and you're good at improvising!

I really don't like being pigeon-holed as an SP. I'm a one-and-only.

Everyone in each of the temperaments is a one-and-only. SPs, however, want to be sure others think of them that way. They tend to prefer center-stage. They are the entertainers, the performers, the salespeople of the world.

I don't always have to be center-stage; sometimes that's not cool. I just don't like to sit back in the corner and miss all the action.

Other SPs share your feelings. They want to leave their mark on the world, but each one wants to do it in his or her own unique way.

Yeah, that's me, but I can't leave a mark if I'm stuck in some old job doing the same thing every day. I keep changing my mind about what I want to do. Sometimes I think I'd like to do something serious, like be a negotiator and solve labor-management disputes. Other times I think I'd rather be a promoter for a rock band. I guess I'd rather not think too far ahead about what I'd like to do.

The characteristic of not planning too far ahead is typical of SPs; however, either choice you mention would be a good one. SPs are good negotiators. They also handle other people well. Unfortunately, SPs usually find sticking to something is hard once they discover the dull, routine aspects of it—and every class in school, every job has some of those. Successful SPs learn ways to get through the boring parts as well as they do the stimulating ones.

That's hard for me. I get A's some days and C's the next, depending on how interesting the work is.

SPs can adapt to any class or, later in life, to any job if they are intrigued by it. What kind of things have been most interesting to you at school?

The best time I've ever had in school was when I had a part in the school play. Before the play was over, all of us who worked on it were really close. We got along great and had a lot of good times.

SPs value belonging to a group as long as there is action, excitement, and variety. This could mean anything from playing in a jazz group or performing on stage to leading a safari of friends to the nearest fast-food oasis. SPs usually have lots of friends in their own age group, but adults of a different temperament may find their behavior annoying. Many adults are uncomfortable with teens acting impulsively. They are afraid such behavior will lead to situations that get out of control.

A lot of adults do get annoyed at me, but I also get around a lot of others. My math teacher, Ms. Brown, gives tons of homework every night and I got tired of that. One day I had done only about a fourth of the

problems, so I put my left arm in a sling. When I handed her my paper, I just raised the "injured" arm, lifted my eyebrows, and smiled. The next day she turned my paper back with no points off for the ones I skipped.

You tell good stories and exceptional lies, too! Those are some ways (and not necessarily good ones) to use the talents of an SP.

So is giving people outrageous compliments at any old time if it gets you off the hook—or even just because you feel like it. You can spot an SP at a party by looking for the person who is telling someone how great they look so that person will wait on them, dance with them—whatever. Remember, we said you'd do well as a negotiator or promoter. Well, it's the same talent. How you use it is up to you.

Are all SPs party people?

That's a good question. No, SPs can enjoy being alone, but most tend to be fun-loving. Remember, we said that they could also be introverts. If they are, they probably amuse themselves by using some special skill they have. They might carve ducks, fix cars, play the piano, or sew, but in a unique way.

Sounds to me like SPs add some pizzazz to the world. So why would anyone not like an SP?

Some people sometimes find some SPs unreliable. Some SPs *can* be unreliable. This may not be true of you, but have you ever made a promise and then not quite carried through with it, then covered up by making an excuse?

Umm...I see what you mean, but look, has this temperament typing stuff got any immediate payoff? I've had about enough talking if it doesn't.

We know that, as an SP, you tend to look for payoffs or you may become cynical about making the effort. One thing you have already got from temperament typing is that you now know more about why you may act the way you do and why others might not always get along with you. After we've described all the different temperaments, we'll suggest ways in which you might want to use this information to help you get along better in school and with other people. Is that enough payoff?

Well, I guess I'm glad I understand my temperament type, but there isn't any reason for me to learn about the others.

One practical reason is that knowledge of the other types will help you give the kind of compliments people really want to hear and you can have more influence over them.

Then that would be worth my time. I'll take a chance on it. Let me skim over the rest of your notes. I don't mind being late for my music lesson.

You certainly sound like an SP! You tend to focus on what's happening *now*. And you try to do what needs to be done in the most expeditious fashion.

But if you tell people you are going to do something or be somewhere, they consider that a commitment. You will be a happier

SP if you are a little more conscious of the consequences of your impulses. For example, do you really have time to skim these notes now and still get to your music lesson? Or do you want to keep your commitment to be on time? And most of all, would the price you pay for being late be worth staying here longer? The choice is yours!

Okay. I hear you. Anything else before I take off? I promise I'll read this stuff later. It really is kind of neat to know why I act the way I do. But for now, I'm outta here!

Chapter Three

SJ
Organizing and Belonging

That which ordinary men are fit for, I am qualified in,
and the best of me is diligence.
William Shakespeare, *King Lear*, I, iv

As with the SP, the **S** means that you like to use your **S**enses of seeing, hearing, feeling, tasting, and smelling to take in facts and information. But the J makes you a very different person from the SP in the ways you deal with the world around you. The **J** means that you tend to use a **J**udging or decision-making process; that is, you like to come to closure and are uncomfortable when situations are open-ended and vague. This combination of characteristics makes you an **SJ** who works hard, doesn't mind following rules, wants to fit in, and pretty much does what your family and teachers expect of you.

I think that's probably what I am. But that makes me sound like a pretty boring person.

Being an SJ doesn't mean being boring. It means you have quieter temperament traits at your core, like enjoying reading. That's far different from being dull.

Even if I'm not dull, I must have some traits you haven't mentioned that make people actually *like* to have me around.

For sure. SJs are generally people who are steady, hardworking, and helpful. The more extroverted ones can be teachers, nurses, grocery clerks, and business owners. SJs tend to be the ones who keep daily life perking along. Most people need stability in their lives and often count on SJs to provide it.

Don't SJs ever relax and just have fun?

Sure. They see excitement as a welcome change of pace—but usually not as a lifestyle. Unexpected change, no matter how much others may think it's fun, can be upsetting to them. SJs like to be invited to a party in plenty of time to get ready, not to be asked at the last minute.

SJs sound like pretty organized people. I'm certainly not totally organized. You should see my closet!

Being an SJ doesn't mean that you have to be compulsively organized about every aspect of your life. Now *that* would make you dull and boring.

However, the traits we've mentioned make SJs valuable members of all types of organizations. Because they can be good team players and enjoy a sense of belonging, they make sure the organization's work gets done, usually quietly, without a lot of fanfare. They also try to be sure other group members do their fair share to help the group function.

You know, I get really upset when people don't carry their weight. My English teacher put a group of six of us to work on a project. Two of us ended up doing all the work and the others, who did almost zip, got the same grade we did.

Many SJs prefer to be responsible for their own work and irresponsibility stresses them. SJs also get stressed when life throws them a curve and doesn't go according to their usually well-laid plans.

I definitely like life to go along smoothly. One of my teachers gave a pop quiz today and I totally panicked. I hate being stressed out by a test I don't have a chance to prepare for.

We bet you're the kind of person who writes assignments and test dates in a notebook and then follows through.

You're right, I do. I'm no scholar, but school isn't hard if you put even a little effort into it.

Most SJs thrive in school because school offers the routines, the customs, and the procedures that make life meaningful for them.

My history teacher said almost the same thing the other day. We asked him why he wanted to be a teacher and he said he likes kids and he also likes school—he can't imagine not teaching American history every year or not hearing the bells ring to change classes or not watching the school teams play on weekends.

Researchers estimate that about 38 percent of the population are SJs, but about 56 percent of teachers are. Why? Because school is itself an organization, and, since SJs like helping others, a profession in education is a natural choice. Since they also like tradition, SJ teachers usually teach in an orderly and organized way—the way they were taught. That suits all the SJ students, but not the SP, NT, and NF students in their classes, who frequently have a rough time with school when their SJ teachers get too structured and routine.

Helping others, wanting life to go along smoothly, not liking big surprises in life—that pretty much describes my folks as well as me. So how does that help me convince them to let me go out next Saturday night?

You might negotiate with them to let you go out as a reward for something they want you to do, like cleaning out the garage. Appeal to their practical side when you ask them: Explain where you plan to go, what you'll do, and with whom. They'll want details about your plans.

I've never gotten into any trouble, but they still give me this long talk about being careful and coming right home if anyone even takes a drink or lights up.

Remember that SJs feel a sense of needing to take care of people. They no doubt feel part of their job as parents is to warn you about possible dangers, like driving or being around kids who are drinking.

If they let you go, keep your part of the deal. Follow through with the plans you told them about. And be in on time. If there are any other rules that they make, follow them, too.

I'm almost always on time, but the other night I came in just a few minutes late and they acted as if I had stayed out all night!

Nothing bothers SJs more than rules that are broken. Even a few minutes matter to most people who are this type.

I can understand why they want me to be on time. What really gets me is that they constantly worry and then complain, like I'm the world's worst kid.

We're afraid that complaining is one way some SJs deal with problems.

Well, they just go on and on about getting into a car accident and this could happen and that could happen and then my mom gets upset and says she has a headache.

You won't change the way they act by being late. You're going to make them complain and worry more and not trust you at all the next time. That's usually the way they are and that's usually how they respond to broken rules. Since you know they are going to fuss, either be on time or, in case of an emergency or even a slip-up, phone them. If you aren't late five times in a row, you might be able to negotiate a reward—like maybe another fifteen minutes!

I guess it's worth a try. My friends aren't troublemakers, either. We just like to get together at the mall and hang out and talk.

Most teens are like you and your friends. That means lots of kids are SJs who have a strong sense of wanting to belong, just like adult SJs. While older SJs belong to clubs and all sorts of associations and business networks, SJ kids enjoy socializing with their own group. These groups may be organized, like scouts or band or cheerleading, or they may be informal, like meeting friends at the mall.

Because these SJ kids—no matter what sort of group they belong to—are responsible people, hanging out doesn't usually mean causing a scene.

Yes, but then something minor happens and some adult says how bad teenagers are!

Now you do sound like an SJ! SJs often look at the gloomy side of life. They tend to believe that if something is going to go wrong, it will.

I do that a lot. I always figure I'd better prepare for the worst. What's going to be is going to be.

Talking and feeling like that is called *fatalism*—a feeling that what happens is predetermined by fate. It's a philosophy common to a lot of SJs.

Kind of like being destined to live with a brother who's a super slob.

Right! And, as you can no doubt guess, disorder is another stressor to the average SJ.

It sure is to me! My brother throws his clothes all over the place and his room is a mess. He won't even listen to our parents. He drives us crazy!

He certainly doesn't sound like an SJ. If you and your parents are SJs, as you say they are, you no doubt drive him crazy, too! In an SJ family, he probably feels like something of an outsider.

I never wondered before if *he* might feel different. Maybe I ought to consider his temperament traits.

Right. When you understand that he isn't deliberately upsetting you but is just being himself, you can let him know why you act the way you do and find some ways to get along more of the time. That's what temperament typing is all about.

Chapter Four

NF
Caring and Questioning

To be or not to be: that is the question.
William Shakespeare, *Hamlet*, III, i

The **N** means that when you take in information, you pay attention to iNtuition—your gut level feeling—rather than relying only on facts and what is observable through your five senses. The **F** means that you make decisions through **F**eeling or values rather than logic and reason. Together, the **NF** characteristics make you a person who is warmhearted, likes people, generally feels upbeat about the future, and constantly searches for ways to understand life, the self, and others.

That's me! I like people. In fact, I've thought about being a teacher. My dad thinks I should go into medicine. Although I want my dad to be proud of what I do, I don't want to spend all my time studying. I hear that's what you have to do to get through medical school.

Do you enjoy activities out of the classroom more than hitting the books?

I sure do. I'm a teacher's aide, belong to the Writer's Club, and am chairperson of a Talent Show committee. We're writing a script that will pull together a group of acts that other students will perform. We've had a lot of fun working on it; it's really going to be great.

Sounds like you're a natural leader.

I tried for class president last year, but the person I ran against was a real slime. I felt that I should say the things that I would do if I won, then trust the class to make the right choice. But he acted as if winning was a matter of life or death. He spent all this money on posters and promised things he couldn't possibly deliver—that's not my style.

NFs tend to have a lot of integrity. To them, the end doesn't always justify the means. They're likely to stand up for principles they believe in, even if they know they may be hurt. In school, NFs aren't usually ones who lie or cheat or break rules.

I think cheating is wrong. But sometimes teachers push kids into it. I have a friend who has had to take care of his little brother, cook, and do a lot around the house because his mother is really sick. When the teacher wouldn't give him another extension, he paid someone to do the report for him. But it's not like he does that all the time; he was backed into a corner.

Yours is a typical NF response. You have integrity, but you also look at a situation and support bending the rules if circumstances warrant it.

Well, I figure nobody's perfect, and I treat people the way I like to be treated.

Anyone special in your life who is treating you the way you like to be treated?

Not right now. Well, there was this person, Chris, who I liked a lot. We went to the homecoming dance together last month and had a great time. But after that Chris sometimes acted as if I were a stranger rather than somebody special and I didn't know what I had done. That really hurt.

What did you do?

I asked Chris to explain what I'd done. Chris started telling me a bunch of stuff that somebody had said about me, none of which was true, but when someone is mad at me, I'm usually just no good at standing up for myself. I get upset and usually feel like crying—anyway, so I walked away. Then Chris tried to make me jealous by hanging around someone else during lunch. I felt really hurt, but I didn't want Chris to know.

So now you...?

Do my own thing at lunch with other friends in another part of the cafeteria. After school I make sure not to go past Chris' locker on my way home or go to any of the places we used to hang out—but now I really want to forget about what happened.

We understand your not wanting to talk about a relationship that was difficult for you. We'd like to point out that your way of responding to Chris' behavior was natural for an NF; that is, you've pulled inward and are closing out the rest of the world for the time being. Being hurt in relationships is hard for NFs, who are usually warm and caring people and want to have close friendships.

I was hurt, but I plan to find some way to make friends with Chris again someday. And I am beginning to get over it. Last night I got on the phone and told several of my friends, in confidence, what Chris did to me.

Making each of your friends feel like they are the one special friend is the kind of behavior that may cause you some problems. People sometimes think that NFs are fickle. Extraverted NFs who get involved with lots of different people often cause others to question the sincerity of their friendship.

There's some truth to that. When I'm one-on-one with someone, that person is all that matters to me—even if I never saw them before. But when I'm with someone else, I concentrate on the new person and I'm annoyed if the first person wants my attention. I don't understand why people can't realize that I try to be there for everyone.

Do you like "being there" for people?

Sure, and I get disgusted when I see other kids putting down people at school who are different or have problems. I wish everyone could just get along with everyone else! I always try to listen and help when other kids talk to me about a problem they have.

That must keep you pretty busy.

It does. Some days I feel people are pulling me in too many different directions.

What do you do then?

I think of some good excuse to tell the ones I don't really like so much that I can't be with them anymore. I try to explain in a way that they won't feel hurt, but it doesn't always work and that makes me feel bad. Generally, I'd rather get a little tired helping others than not be there for them.

Do the people who tell you their problems take your advice?

I don't give a lot of advice because most people just want somebody to talk to. Earlier this week, one girl told me about some problems she was having with her parents. I didn't say anything that would be very helpful, but when she left she said I was a "truly special person." That made me feel great all day—like I really am somebody special!

NFs are good at sensing how others feel. On the other hand, they are also constantly searching for their unique identity and like being praised. But they usually have more trouble handling negative criticism than the other three temperaments.

That's me, too! Last month my English teacher put a group of six of us to work on a poetry project. There was one kid in our group who had trouble reading. Since I enjoy poetry, I helped him, but one of the other kids in the group made comments about how stupid I was to do somebody else's work. That really hurt.

We can understand why you felt upset when someone didn't understand and appreciate your gesture of helpfulness. The person who made the negative comments was probably not an NF. Look at the situation from another point of view. That person might feel that you were being phony and *too* helpful.

That person also may not have liked working with a group and was annoyed with the entire poetry project; making negative comments was a way of complaining and venting annoyance. Although extraverted NFs enjoy group work, or what teachers call *cooperative learning,* others may not. How did you feel about the experience?

It made English class seem more like an after-school meeting. I hate it when the teacher does nothing but lecture. Except for the comments that one kid made, I enjoyed the group work. Even though two people wrote most of the report, we all contributed.

What was your role in the group?

I was really pleased with my part. The others were arguing, which I hate, so I suggested a topic and convinced the others to choose it.

Most NFs are good at communication. Some of our finest writers and speakers—people like Shakespeare and Martin Luther King—seem to have been NFs.

I've decided I must be an NF since I've got most of the characteristics that you've said NFs have. One thing puzzles me, though....I have a friend who is a lot like me, but, even though I like going out on weekends, he usually stays home. He definitely doesn't enjoy parties. Does that mean he isn't an NF?

No, even though most NFs like people, many of them, especially the more introverted ones, may not be party-people. They can have a genuine warmth toward others but still value their privacy and prefer activities on their own or with one or two close friends.

That sounds like my friend. He likes getting together with me at one of our houses. When we talk, we let our imagination roam a lot, daydreaming about what can be done this way and what that way—really low-key stuff. Mom complains that we waste a lot of time.

Remember Martin Luther King, who said, "I have a dream." He was a true visionary, an NF who acted on his dream of a better world.

Wow! The next time my mother criticizes me for daydreaming, I'll tell her that dreamers like me have important contributions to make. That'll make her happy.

That's an NF line for sure!

Chapter Five

NT
Understanding
and Knowing

Suit the action to the word, the word to the action.
William Shakespeare, *Hamlet,* III, ii

As with the NF, the **N** indicates that you like to use iNtuition when you collect information rather than relying only on facts and what you observe. The **T** says you are a **T**hinker who reasons and studies a situation before you make a decision. If you are an **NT,** this combination means you tend to pride yourself on the way you think—logically, rationally, and intelligently—and you like to learn for the sake of learning.

That does describe me, but I sound like some wise old owl who sits around all day going, "Hmmm-mm."

Funny you should say that because some of the people who study and write about temperament typing use an owl to represent the NT. Some also call the NT the Rational, which implies being reasonable and logical.

Others have compared the NT to Prometheus. Prometheus was the

Greek god who stole fire from Mount Olympus and gave it to humans; like Prometheus, NTs generally want to have power and to understand and control the world they live in.

If they're into power, then I may not be an NT. I'm not a kid who dreams of making millions and being a corporate bigshot.

Ah, but that may mean you *are* an NT. We said that NTs are into learning for the sake of learning. They are generally competent in their work, but they do it for *themselves,* for self-gratification. They relish the power they feel inside by having done a good job more than the power that comes from earning lots of money or having a position of status. How does that definition of power fit you?

That sounds more like me. My teachers are always saying that I could make all A's if I put my mind to it.

So why don't you? You seem smart enough.

Getting straight A's doesn't really matter to me. I mean, I'd like to show my folks a report card with great grades, but I'd rather spend my time doing things that are important to me. I don't have time for the boring stuff that teachers expect us to do.

Do you have any teachers you like because they don't give you boring assignments?

There's one teacher I get along with really well. I like to stop by her room after school to talk and bounce around ideas for school projects I'm doing. I actually get along better with her than I do with most kids.

Why do you get along so well with her?

Because she listens to me and treats me like an adult. Most teachers talk to me like a kid who's bothering them with dumb questions.

Because NT kids tend to be serious and thoughtful, they frequently feel more comfortable with adults, especially those who respect their intellectual curiosity, than they feel with other students. Do you have many friends your own age?

Not many. I feel really comfortable around very few people, although sometimes I do enjoy parties.

Let's assume that most people feel comfortable around people who are similar to them. One reason some NTs may feel uncomfortable around others is that NTs make up only seven to twelve percent of our population. That means that at a party of twenty people, probably only two others are NTs. If one or both of them are introverts and you are an extrovert, you won't have anyone very much like you at the party! In a class of thirty-two, statistically you'll find three to four NTs and three to four NFs, compared with about twelve SPs and twelve SJs. Of course, as they say, actual rates may vary.

**Part of my problem in getting along with other kids
is that they seem so stupid sometimes. In history class,
for example, my teacher asks interesting questions that
make us think. Even though there are no right or wrong
answers, some of the kids make ridiculous comments.
They waste everyone's time.**

NTs tend to enjoy complex discussions that help them make
sense of the world. We're sure other NTs have the same problem in
classes that you do. What else that's important to you is happening in
school?

**My English teacher assigned us a research topic. We
don't have to write the whole paper, I'm happy to say
—just make note cards and an outline and write an
introduction. I liked that. Why write it all out anyway?**

Sometimes writing material out helps a person organize thoughts
and clarify ideas.

**Sorry, but that doesn't make sense to me. Spending a
lot of time typing what's already written on notecards
would be a huge waste of time. I'd probably never get
it done.**

You're lucky to have an English teacher who thinks the way you
do! What was your topic?

**I picked earthquakes. I found out what causes them, how
the Richter scale was developed, and why scientists are**

predicting a major quake in the Midwest within the next twenty years. That kind of information was so interesting to me that I made *hundreds* of note cards.

Sounds like you did a good job organizing to get all that information down on cards and whip it into an outline.

Right, I was organized in this case. But I'm not always that way. My locker at school is a mess, and you should see my room at home! I never seem to find the time to clean up because there are other things I'd rather be doing.

What kind of things do you like to do?

Sports, reading, lots of things. What I *don't* like is routine. Like my mom insists on a big Sunday dinner every week. We always have roast chicken, mashed potatoes, and cake or pie for dessert. We use cloth napkins and she makes my little sister say a prayer before dinner.

NTs are generally not into observances and ritual. Because they usually want reasons for doing something, they're not big on the idea of tradition.

Your mother may be an SJ. Many SJs cherish tradition. They not only enjoy group traditions, like a Christmas dinner or a Channukah celebration, but they may also start and perpetuate their own family traditions because they value opportunities to pull friends and relatives together.

Don't talk about relatives! Last Sunday I was reading a book when Mom interrupted me. Some cousins were visiting. That seemed like a trivial reason to break into what I was involved with. When I finally got back to my book, I couldn't remember where I was and I wasted more time rereading part of it.

Did you tell your mom how you felt about being interrupted?

No. It was late when everyone left so I just shrugged it off. I didn't want to start anything up again.

What do you mean by "again"?

Several days ago my sister was in the bathroom for over an hour and left it a mess. Mom told her to clean it. She eventually did, but later when I said something, they both turned on me and acted as if the whole thing was my fault.

What did you say?

I asked if Her Majesty could limit her beauty practices.

And then?

Mom said that I should let the matter drop, mind my own business, and stop being so critical and sarcastic.

Being critical and sarcastic unfortunately comes easily to NTs, but other people are often hurt by biting words.

Did your sister say anything about your being sarcastic?

My sister said that she had cleaned the bathroom. Then she said that I should keep my own room clean. That last comment was completely off-base, since I have to use the bathroom but she doesn't have to even enter my room.

Did you tell her that?

No, because there was no way I could even come close to winning in that situation. So I went to my room and read. Reading helps when I'm upset.

Has your sister kept her bathroom time limited since then and cleaned up after herself when she's done?

Most of the time. I think Mom felt bad about the whole thing because she congratulated me at dinner for taking out the trash before being asked. That's my job. It was so obviously ridiculous for her to say anything that I felt embarrassed.

Sounds like you don't like to get compliments.

Not if I don't deserve it…. And sometimes if I *do* deserve it! I get uneasy with that kind of personal stuff. Some people have told me I'm cold and kind of distant. I don't feel that I am. I just don't fall all over people, complimenting them so they have to compliment me back. That's being false.

You could try complimenting your sister when she doesn't stay too long in the bathroom. Lots of people, especially SJs and NFs, respond positively to praise.

Why compliment her on something she should do anyway? And I did thank her one time.

When was that?

Several months ago, but how often do I have to tell her? It seems to me that once is enough. She can't expect me to shower her with praise for a short shower!

We'll ignore the pun and just say that most NTs feel the same way you do about giving and receiving compliments and kudos. Have you been aware of this aspect of your temperament at some other time?

Yes. Last spring I was going with someone named Pat, who asked almost every day how I felt about going together. How I felt was really uncomfortable—because of having to say it, even though we had a great time with each other.

Just as NTs tend to find it hard to offer praise, they usually find it difficult to express their feelings to people, no matter how deeply they may care for them.

We eventually broke up, but it wasn't because I didn't care. Pat misinterpreted my answers to the constant prying if I was happy and in love. The relationship

wasn't worth the hassle. My mother sometimes hugs me and says "I love you," and I feel uncomfortable about that, too.

You are like many NTs. If someone you are close to forces the issue, you can probably say "I love you" when pushed, but you may feel that you're choking on the words. Yet others who are not NTs can easily say "I love you" to someone—even those who may not always mean it!

So I guess if I want someone who appreciates me the way I am, I have to find another NT?

Not necessarily. Even if NTs aren't into *complimenting,* people of different temperaments can *complement* each other. Remember at the beginning we said no one temperament type is superior to another? If you now understand yourself better, you'll be better able to explain to someone else why you act as you do. And better able to understand why they act as they do. Vive la différence!

Chapter Six

Making the Best of Yourself in School

We know what we are, but know not what we may be.
William Shakespeare, *Hamlet,* IV, v

By now you should have a pretty good idea what your temperament type might be:

- If you're an **SP,** you're probably asking, "So what's the big deal! What good is all this to me?"

- If you're an **SJ,** you're probably asking, "How can I use this idea now that I know about it?"

- If you're an **NF,** you're probably asking, "How can this help me work with others?"

- If you're an **NT,** you're probably asking, "Where can I find out more about temperament typing?"

Hey, that one comment is pretty close to what I was thinking!

In this chapter, let's talk about how knowing your temperament can help you with your schoolwork. We'll talk about all four temperaments. Let's discuss each one in the order we talked about them before: SP, SJ, NF, and then NT.

The way you described an SP earlier, it sounded as if the SP will never be very good in school.

Absolutely not so. It's just that SPs tend to do things their own way. They can get bored so easily that school can be a real drag, but they can be very successful if given a lot of freedom and some structure and consistent limits by an understanding teacher and other school staff. The SP who is always bucking authority is his or her own worst enemy. The SP who uses the classroom as a stage and ridicules a teacher or makes the teacher look stupid or ignorant is setting up a situation where the teacher will be forced to dispense punishment. Moreover, since grades are not absolutes, a student who really annoys a teacher is not likely to get a break from that teacher at grading time.

In their own best interests, SP students can:

- Try to take courses from teachers that everyone says are interesting and exciting and have clear goals

- Pick hands-on courses like art, shop, band, or drama for electives

- Choose term paper topics that are unusual, different, and interesting

- If extraverted, ask to present papers orally

- Do their hardest, most unliked homework first—or they'll never get to it!

- If extraverted, have a parent or friend check homework for details

- If introverted, use a checklist to be sure everything is neat and complete

What can an SP do to get along better with other people in class?

Since SPs are good at coming up with exciting ideas and getting things started, they could help class projects get underway.

They are also good at trouble-shooting, so they can help when a class project bogs down. But they must pull their weight on the project right away—something they tend not to do—or others in the class will resent their jumping in.

SPs often have interesting ideas to contribute to class discussions. But extravert SPs have to be careful not to dominate the whole show and turn the classroom into a stage on which they perform—especially as the class clowns.

Would an SP make a good leader—president of the student government, for example?

An SP would make a good student government president, especially for a school with poor school spirit and minimal interest in student projects and programs. An SP in that situation could stir kids up and inspire a lot of action.

But an SP might have less luck in a school that honored a lot of traditions or one where the teachers prefer to control the student government. If an SP wanted to be a leader in that school, he or she might try out for a part in the school play and leave SJs to run the student government.

Okay. What about SJs? They must love school.

They often do. SJs generally do just fine in school because they tend to follow the rules, keep track of homework, get to class on time, and get along with their teachers—lots of whom are SJs!

Is there anything SJs should watch out for?

SJs will do their very best if they:

- Select teachers who give facts and are clear about what theywant the students to learn

- Select teachers who lecture and have a syllabus

- Use the library, including its information retrieval systems

- Learn how to use audiovisual equipment and computers

- If introverted, find a quiet place to do homework where no one will disturb them

- If extraverted, do homework with a study buddy who is also an extravert SJ and shares scholastic goals

- Solve problems by applying and adapting efforts that worked before to the new problem

- Understand that every failure isn't the end of the world

- Try to be less vocal in criticism of classmates, if extraverted

- If introverted, realize that body language as much as words can show intolerance toward classmates

If they like school and aren't tolerant of others, don't most kids who aren't SJs dislike them?

SJs don't have to be disliked. They can get along fine with others if they learn to act friendly and not brag. They have to be especially careful not to be sarcastic and critical of others who don't happen to follow the rules or make the grades the way they do. They also have to remember that there's more to schoolwork than just memorizing. They have to accept others who question facts and ideas and traditions. That doesn't mean they have to agree to these ideas—just think about them. They also have to learn that even people who don't play by the rules often have good ideas worth listening to.

Teachers must love SJs.

Usually, but not always. An NF English teacher would probably go crazy with an SJ student who didn't like poetry and who was interested in only the basic plot when reading novels.

Would an SJ make a good president of the student government?

In most schools, absolutely, and most SJs would love the title of president. Student council meetings would be on time. Old school traditions would be carried on and even strengthened. Reports would be turned in and projects finished—provided the SJ had learned to respect and get along with fellow classmates. If not, the other students would fail to follow his or her leadership and the president would turn the job into a disaster.

What about NFs? Do they like school or not?

With NFs it all depends on the teacher. They can be so people-oriented that a teacher who responds to them personally can get them to love school, but a teacher who is critical and impersonal can turn them off completely.

NFs need to remember these things about school:

- Try to see the motives and goodness of teachers who don't necessarily act warm and friendly

- Roll with the punch if they don't get the grade they expect; they shouldn't take it as a personal cut by the teacher

- Distract themselves and not dwell on their disappointment at not getting approval for work done

- Realize that not all teachers play fair; that's just the way the world is

- Consider giving an oral report if extraverted, whenever a teacher allows a choice

- In making either written or oral reports, thoroughly research the topic and be prepared with good facts and figures to support ideas

- Choose a buddy who is smart in a subject causing the NF trouble. Extravert NFs can constructively share study time if the time is not spent socializing

- Ask a super-organized friend for help in developing a good organization system; then follow it

- Study alone, if introverted

- Read a good book on a subject being studied in class

- Set deadlines to help finish work of minimal interest

What about NFs and how they get along with others?

That's the least of their worries! They like people and generally people like them because they are good listeners. They are likely to be good group workers, and the group helps them do their best, but they can study alone just as well if they have to.

Whether introverted or extroverted, NFs tend to want harmony when with other people. Because schools are filled with people, lots of NFs enjoy going to school, where they try to be pleasant and helpful to teachers and other students.

I know a girl who sounds like an NF. She's a teacher's pet, trying to help all the time. Many of the kids say that little NF is a real pain.

Other types may find the NF's desire for harmony and helpfulness annoying. In class discussion where facts and ideas are the important focus, NFs may also get others annoyed because, rather than talking about ideas, they deal with the emotions of the people who are talking about the ideas.

The NF's biggest problem, however, is that they tend to take on all the troubles of their classmates and can end up stressing themselves out.

Would an NF make a good class president?

Under an NF, there would probably be lots of parties and peace rallies and charity dances. They might well lose the financial records, but they would chip in with their own money to make up any deficit.

But if the NF had to work with an NT or SJ principal, things might not go too well. The NF would want lots of praise for accomplishments, praise that NTs generally don't feel it necessary to give. The NF would try to soft-soap the principal into getting what he or she felt was good for the school and, in doing so, the principal would probably be thoroughly antagonized. The SJ principal would respect only facts and figures and an NF might not be inclined to provide them.

You haven't talked about NTs. Do they get good grades in school?

They often do if the content of the class interests them. Usually, they are not so interested in learning what the *teacher* says they should learn as what *they* think they should. If you want a study partner, someone who will help you do well on a test, make friends with an NT who feels the material is relevant and worth learning!

But NTs have things to remember, too, if they want to do their best in school. They should consider these things:

- Choose teachers who are content centered, especially teachers who are good lecturers

- Avoid incompetent teachers

- If an incompetent teacher can't be avoided, remember not to blow a grade by not doing homework or not studying for a test

- Be careful not to lose patience and destroy what has been done after messing up a math problem—relax and carefully, slowly check the steps and find the error

- If a lab partner isn't doing his or her share of the work, confront the partner; don't wait until the end of the semester when it's too late to clear the air. An introvert might prefer to ask the teacher to intervene

- Realize that filling in forms and paperwork for the school administration has to be done. It doesn't always make sense, but one usually saves time by just doing it

- Failing is not the worst thing that can happen. Don't drop a class for fear of not making an A in it

- If failure happens, recover self-esteem by taking on a new project

- When feeling overwhelmed by tasks, break big jobs down into little ones

- If extraverted, consider developing a mentor relationship with a favorite teacher

What do they need to do to get along better with fellow students?

Oftentimes, a lot! NTs need to learn how to talk with others about what those students like. NTs can give the impression that they don't care about other people.

If NTs quote statistics and catch on quickly in class discussions, they can make other students look dumb. Not that they should keep quiet! They need to consider how they sound and modify their comments to avoid sounding pompous.

Similarly, NTs who want to make a point in class about an error made by a teacher or student need to do it with humor. Otherwise, people will take it as a personal criticism and think them cruel when they are not. They must also not be so intent on their own learning that they forget to help others do their best.

Would an NT make a good class president?

NTs love power. An extrovert NT president could run the show and probably do it very well. The job would be done efficiently, that's for sure. The president might start some new school competitions. But if a school had a valued tradition that had no basis and seemed silly to the NT, the NT president might not go along with it and then would antagonize others, especially SJs.

A friend of mine is really turned off by school. He is always talking about dropping out. Can knowing about temperament typing help him?

You bet. The drive, or motivation, to do anything, including getting out of bed and going to school or a job, depends on a person's finding some element of school or the job that appeals to his or her temperament needs. There are at least two things your friend can do if he knows his type.

The first thing he should do is locate some adult at school who is the same type he is—anyone, whether a teacher, the principal, a cafeteria worker, or a coach. That person will truly understand him when he talks about his problems with school. He should make a point of seeing that person every day. For an introvert, that may take a bit of courage, but it's worth it.

That person may also be able to help him with step two. The second thing he can do is try to find some element—something that meets one of his deepest temperament needs—he can look forward to every day. A schedule change to a class that allows him to be creative and work with his hands may motivate him. Even better if he can find something he looks forward to doing in every class he takes. This may be no more than keeping all the books on the reference shelf organized in each classroom, if organization is a key temperament need. Or maybe jotting down one idea he gets from a class, even if that idea comes from another student and has nothing at all to do with the content of the class. Perhaps a few minutes of time to daydream on his own will solve his problem.

Dropping out is not your friend's answer. *Tuning in* to his basic needs in life and how they can be met at school will help him in the long run.

Those ideas might make school more fun for me, too, even though I'm not about to drop out.

For sure. A key element to being happy in this life is knowing what things or people or events truly make you feel good about yourself. When you know your true needs, you can set your life goals to meet those needs. You are uniquely you, and only you can know the particular balance of needs and goals that you must strive for to feel fulfilled. Knowing your temperament type is simply a start in identifying these needs and goals.

I think I've figured out what type I am, but I'm not sure.

One way you can quickly find out more about your temperament and type is by taking the *Myers-Briggs Type Indicator*® (MBTI®). Many guidance counselors and other people who work in the field of human behavior are trained to give the MBTI. It is a set of questions about preferences. Taking it is easy and doesn't take long, and the results will give you information about which one of sixteen types you are. The MBTI can add to the information you get from this book to help you with the important task of confirming what your temperament is and how best to act on it.

If by acting on it you mean getting along with other people, I need to know more about how to do it.

Let's talk about it.

Chapter Seven

Finding the Best in Others

It is a wise child that knows his own father.
Homer
It is a wise father that knows his own child.
William Shakespeare

There are so many people in your life that it would be impossible for you to know the temperament type of each one, but you can benefit from figuring out the types of those people who are most important to you—your family, your close friends, and your teachers (and your rivals, if you have any). The more you know about their temperaments, the more easily you can communicate with them.

I've already tried figuring out my mom's type, and I was confused. She sometimes seems like one temperament and other times another. How do I know which one she is?

If you think you can get your mom interested, have her read this book and let *her* tell you which description seems to fit her best. What she will most likely tell you is that she was one way when she was a child, began to change in her teens, then changed to her present temperament as an adult. Some people are consistent and remain close to their temperament from infancy on into adulthood. Other people, because of pressures of family or circumstances, have to let it evolve. If this is the case with your mom, she may indeed be able to act as if she is two or more different types, depending on what's happening to her at the time.

How can she shift back and forth if temperament is so fundamental to the person?

Haven't you ever noticed that when you are sick you often act much younger? You want special foods and don't mind some expressions of affection that you might normally find embarrassing.

That's true.

You are reverting to an earlier life stage. You might notice if your mother behaves differently when she doesn't feel well or is upset. That's when many of us go back to earlier behaviors.

But there is such a difference between her two temperaments, I don't know which one to respond to.

Learn to respond to both. You need to think about how her temperaments seem to vary and how to respond, depending on which she is showing. For example, if she is acting like an NF, and you want permission to go to a party, act sociable. Take her out for a burger and tell her about the party and the other people going. Ask her about the parties she went to when she was your age. On the other hand, if she is in an NT mood, prepare a careful statement of what you want to do, why you want to do it, who will be there, and when you will return.

Be prepared to answer lots of "why" questions. If she is acting like an adult SJ, don't even think of asking about going to the party until you have done all your chores, have your homework up to date, and can show some good grades. If she is feeling like an SP, all you probably need to do is tell her how excited you are about the party—your biggest problem may be keeping her from going with you!

That somehow sounds like I'm being phony....

Not at all, because what you are trying to do is to convey your request in the way that it is most likely to be understood by your mother. She still may not permit you to go, but if you do not convey your request in a way that she understands, she may refuse to let you go—not because she has good reasons, but because she didn't understand you. If she understands, she may let you go.

I wish my mom understood me better so I wouldn't have to try to figure her out. Getting along with my dad is a lot easier. I think we must be the same temperament.

Parents tend to think that all their children will have the same temperament they do. If a child turns out to be different, they have a harder time understanding that child than they do the child who is the same type they are.

What about teachers? How can temperament typing help me get along better with them?

Consider how knowing temperament types will help you in preparing a report. The NF teacher will probably be most interested in a personal, anecdotal report. An NT teacher will probably prefer a thoughtful, detailed report. An SJ teacher will no doubt want a well-documented, factual report that follows all the rules of composition. An SP teacher will likely prefer something original and won't care if you break the rules. So when you write a report, keep in mind the temperament type of the teacher.

What about class discussions? The same thing?

Absolutely! Be sure to speak up in an SJ teacher's class and be clear about what you have to say. Better not to go off into long personal stories. Those stories will probably work better in an NF teacher's class. If you can't give concrete facts and back them up, you might be better off keeping quiet in an NT teacher's class until you can prepare your remarks. And if you like being the class comic and are quick-witted, save your best remarks for the SP teacher's class.

But how do I figure out what temperament type a teacher is?

Here we can give you only some very general ideas that you can use in addition to the information we've already talked about. An SP teacher, for example, could be more easily distracted from a planned lesson and would enjoy an impromptu discussion. An SJ teacher is usually concerned with details and facts and is very organized. An NT teacher would most likely be concerned with theories and ask "why" questions. An NF teacher would probably try to teach on a personal level and perhaps be more willing to listen to reasons for not getting an assignment in on time. He or she might not accept the reason, but *would* be very empathetic!

Here's an important BUT: These are *only* generalizations. Remember that typing someone, whether yourself, a teacher, a parent, or a friend, is a matter of constantly checking out your impressions and revising them and confirming your observations.

Remember, too, that even people whom we think we know very well, like close friends, may do things that are unexpected and seemingly out of character.

Can we talk some more about friends? I like this person who is clearly very different from me. We have some awful arguments, but we keep on being friends. Then there's another person I can't stand but this person seems to be very much like me. How can that be?

You have touched on a really important aspect of temperament typing. Many times we are attracted to people who are opposite from us because they can do and be things we wish we could do or be. For example, an SP can bring spontaneity and fun into the life of an SJ friend and the NT can explain income tax regulations to the NF when the NF is totally at a loss!

Paradoxically, we can dislike someone who is very much like us because they behave in ways that make us see ourselves all too clearly. They show us sides of ourselves that we are ashamed of or embarrassed about or afraid of. Part of growing up is learning to accept who you are and making the most of it—knowing you can never be perfect.

Then are you saying that it takes *all* the types to make the world go round?

Exactly. We balance each other out. If we learn to get along with *all* people, our lives will be enhanced and so will theirs.

Selected Resources

Farris, D. *Type Tales.* Palo Alto, CA: Consulting Psychologists Press, 1990.

Giovannoni, L., Berens, L. V. and Cooper, S. A. *Introduction to Temperament.* Huntington Beach, CA: Telos Publications, 1988.

Hirsh, S. and Kummerow, J. M. *LifeTypes.* New York: Warner Books, 1989.

Keirsey, D. and Bates, M. *Please Understand Me.* Del Mar, CA: Prometheus Nemesis Books, 1978.

Lawrence, G. *People Types and Tiger Stripes: A Practical Guide to Learning Styles.* Gainesville, FL: Center for Applications of Psychological Type, Inc., 1979.

Murphy, E., and Meisgeier, C. *Murphy-Meisgeier Type Indicator for Children.* Palo Alto, CA: Consulting Psychologists Press, 1989.

Myers, I. B. with Myers, P. *Gifts Differing.* Palo Alto, CA: Consulting Psychologists Press, 1990, 1980.